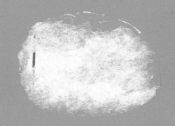

CREATURES
OF THE DEEP

Design
David West
Children's Book Design
Illustrations
Aziz Khan
Picture Research
Cecilia Weston-Baker
Editor
Scott Steedman
Consultant
Miles Barton

Designed and produced by
Aladdin Books Ltd
70 Old Compton Street
London W1V 5PA

First Published in
Great Britain in 1989 by
Franklin Watts
12a Golden Square
London W1

ISBN 0 86313 974 4

Printed in Belgium

This book tells you about animals from the depths of the oceans – what they eat, where they live and how they survive. Find out some surprising facts about them in the boxes on each page. The identification chart at the back of the book will help you when you see creatures of the deep in an aquarium or marine park.

The little squares show you how big the animal is, compared to a person.

The picture opposite shows a snaggletooth, a carnivorous deep-sea fish

FIRST SIGHT
CREATURES OF THE DEEP
Lionel Bender

GLOUCESTER PRESS
London · New York · Toronto · Sydney

Introduction

Two-thirds of the Earth's surface is covered by water. Most of this water is in seas and oceans, which are very deep in places. Some underwater trenches reach 6.5 km (4.2 miles) below sea level. In the open seas, sunlight only penetrates the top 200m (650ft) of water. As plants need sunlight, they cannot grow any deeper. Below this "light zone", it gets increasingly dark and there is less food for animals to eat. Beyond 1,800m (6,000ft) there is hardly a glimmer of light. At these depths the pressure of the water is immense – a person would be crushed instantly.

Many animals that live in deep water have bizarre shapes, structures and behaviours. This is because they must be adapted to survive in darkness, without live plant food and under great pressure.

Contents

◁ **The fearsome head of an Angler Fish**

Ocean depths

Animals live at all depths of the oceans, though they become fewer as you descend. Differences in light, pressure and the amount of salt in the water create distinct natural zones. The upper zone contains the greatest number and variety of fish. The surface waters are also rich in invertebrates (animals without backbones) like octopuses, lobsters and jellyfish.

Marine mammals, such as whales, and reptiles, such as turtles, dive deep in the oceans. But they must return to the surface regularly to breathe. Some 2,000 species of fish, including the Angler and Lantern Fish, spend their whole lives in the depths. On the ocean floor live burrowing worms, Sea Cucumbers, sponges and shellfish.

Sea Cucumbers are found on the ocean floor

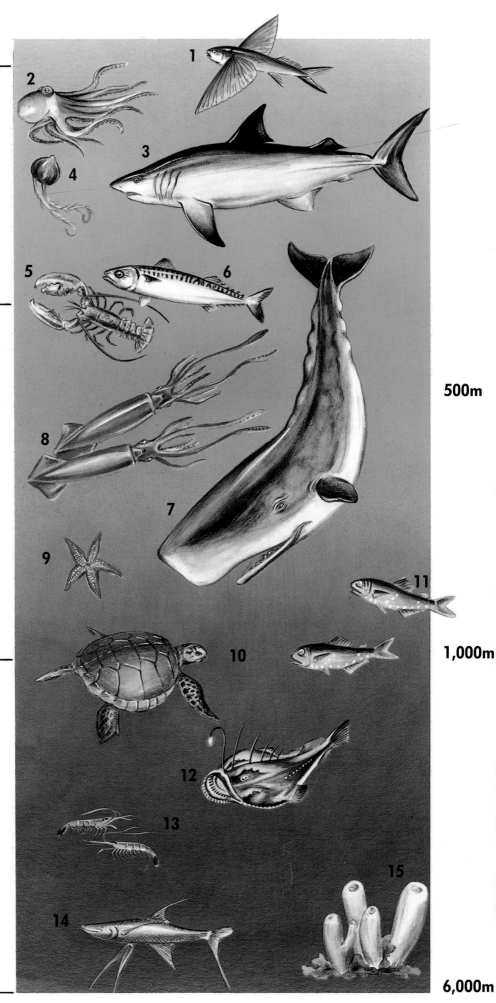

1. **Flying Fish**
2. **Octopus**
3. **Great White Shark**
4. **Sea Gooseberry**
5. **Lobster**
6. **Mackerel**
7. **Sperm Whale**
8. **Squid**
9. **Starfish**
10. **Turtle**
11. **Lantern Fish**
12. **Angler Fish**
13. **Deep-sea Shrimp**
14. **Tripod Fish**
15. **Sea Sponge**

Euphotic zone

Bathyal zone

Abyssal zone

500m

1,000m

6,000m

The top zone of the ocean is the euphotic zone. This zone ends where light can no longer penetrate the water. Beneath it are the bathyal and abyssal zones. At night, some midwater animals swim to the surface to feed. Deep-water animals rarely leave the abyssal zone.

Food chains

There are no plants living in the ocean depths. But all creatures of the deep ultimately depend on plants for their survival. Plants use the energy of sunlight to make their own food. Animals cannot do this. Instead they get their energy by eating plants, other animals, or both. Tiny free-floating plants called phytoplankton form the base of every marine food chain. Phytoplankton grow and multiply in the surface waters. They are eaten by invertebrates and fish. These are preyed upon in turn by larger fish, such as sharks, and by other predators like squid and whales.

When these plants and animals die, their remains fall to the bottom of the ocean. This "rain" of food is eaten by the scavengers of the deep, which include Sea Cucumbers, shrimps and Fan Worms. Predators – the hunters of the deep – feed on the scavengers and on each other.

Deep-sea shrimp use their claws to seize large pieces of food

The Great White Shark often hunts for smaller fish in deep water ▷

Big and small

In 1878 a Giant Squid 16.6m (55ft) long was found stranded on a beach in Newfoundland. It weighed two tonnes. This species lives at depths down to 600m (2,000ft), where it hunts and eats fish, shellfish and other squid. It is the world's largest soft-bodied animal. But even it is dwarfed by the Sperm Whale, which can grow to 20m (68ft) and weigh 70 tonnes. It mainly preys on squid. The complete body of a 12m (39ft) Giant Squid has been found in a Sperm Whale's stomach.

Probably the most common fish in the ocean are the Bristlemouths. These live 500m (1,650ft) or more beneath the surface, where they feed on small shellfish. Bristlemouths are tiny – each one is smaller than your thumb. Together with the equally small Hatchet and Lantern Fish, they make up 90 per cent of all deep-sea predators.

Oarfish

The Oarfish has a body like a ribbon and a head shaped like that of a horse. If a person could dive deep enough, he would be tiny next to this 9m (30ft) long fish. We believe that Oarfish feed on shellfish. Almost nothing else is known about its habits.

Two tiny deep-sea predators, a Lantern Fish (above) and a Hatchet Fish ▷

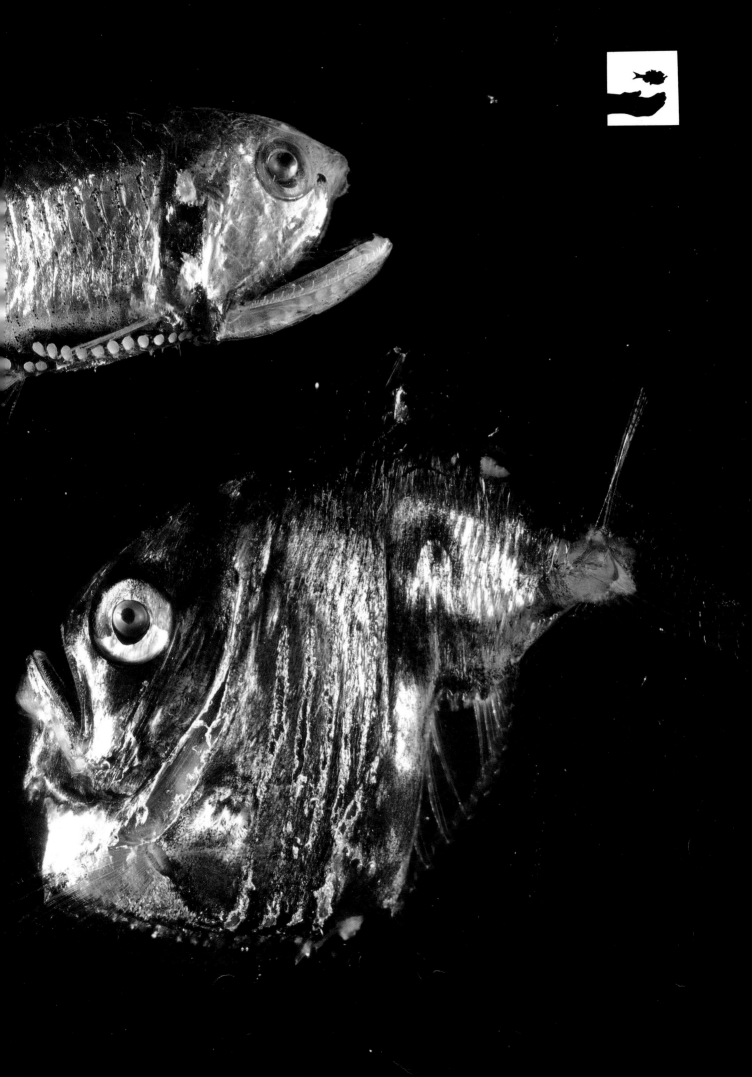

Huge jaws

Swallowers, gulpers, loosejaws, snaggletooths and dragons – these are just some of the names given to deep-sea fish. All these animals have huge gaping mouths and fearsome teeth. Because it is impossible to search for food in the darkness, they swim along with their mouths wide open, ready to gobble up anything edible that comes along. Sometimes, their victim is one of their own kind – by accident they are cannibals.

Swallowers and Viper Fish are about 15cm (6in) long. They can gobble up prey twice their own size. Their huge jaws, lined with curved, fang-like teeth, take up most of their heads. The fish use their teeth to stab prey and pull it into their mouths. When they swallow, their heads appear to become separated from their bodies. Their stomachs can stretch enormously, as if they were made of elastic. A large meal may keep a Viper Fish going for several days.

Viper Fish

During the day Viper Fish feed in the deepest waters. At night they migrate towards the surface, where the fish they prey on are more common. It is also easier for them to escape their predators in the dark of night. These include whales and sharks.

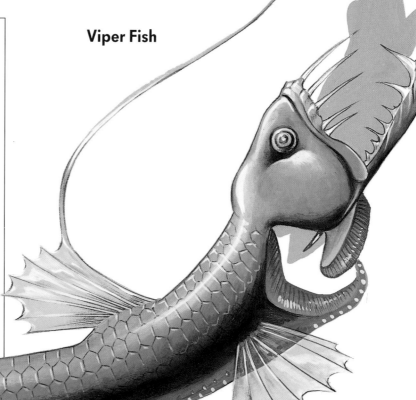

12

A Gulper Eel waits for a meal to swim by ▷

Devils of the dark

Skates, rays and chimaeras are all relatives of sharks. They live as far as 2.4 km (1.5 miles) below the ocean's surface. These fish are often compared to devils, because they can produce nasty poisons and powerful electric shocks.

The Atlantic Torpedo Ray feeds on other fish. It stuns its prey with electric shocks produced near the tips of its "wings". Its close relative, the Pacific Big Skate, is equally vicious. Its tail is long and thin and is covered with sharp thorns. When threatened, it whips its tail forward and strikes these against its attacker. One species of chimaera, the Ratfish, has a poisonous spine on top of its head. This can inflict a painful wound.

The Rat-tail Fish uses its sharp spines to warn off predators

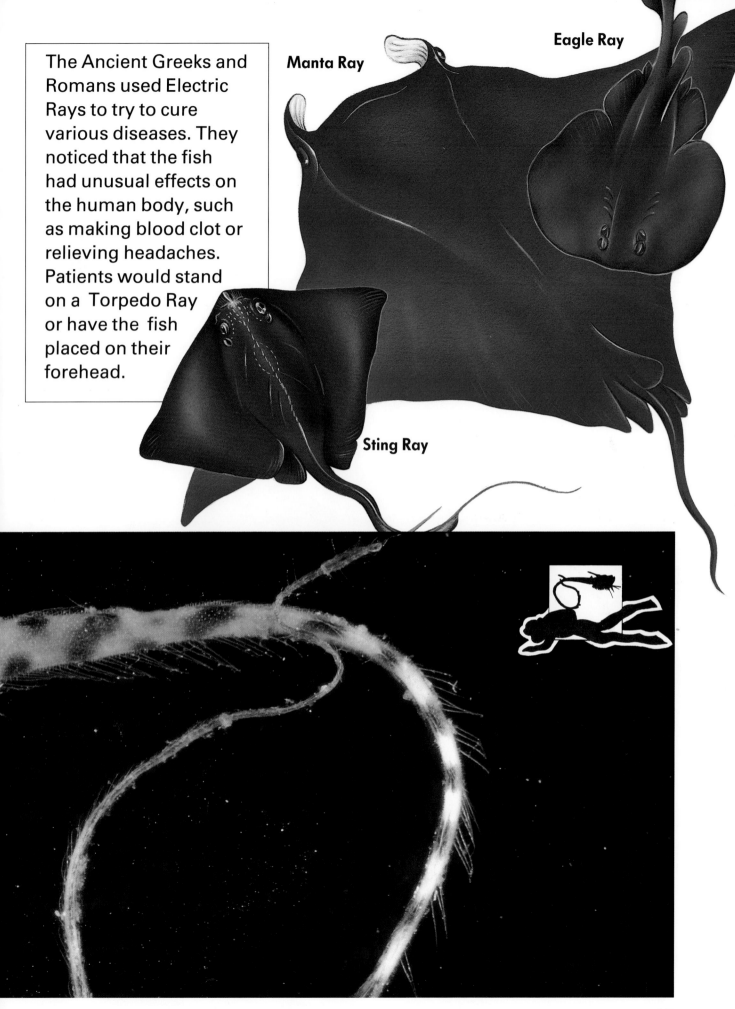

The Ancient Greeks and Romans used Electric Rays to try to cure various diseases. They noticed that the fish had unusual effects on the human body, such as making blood clot or relieving headaches. Patients would stand on a Torpedo Ray or have the fish placed on their forehead.

Manta Ray

Eagle Ray

Sting Ray

Angler Fish may produce up to 2 million eggs at a time. These float to the ocean surface in a jelly-like mass. The larvae that hatch from the eggs swim deeper as they grow. Any males that fail to find a female soon die. Once they have bitten into a female, the males will live on her blood.

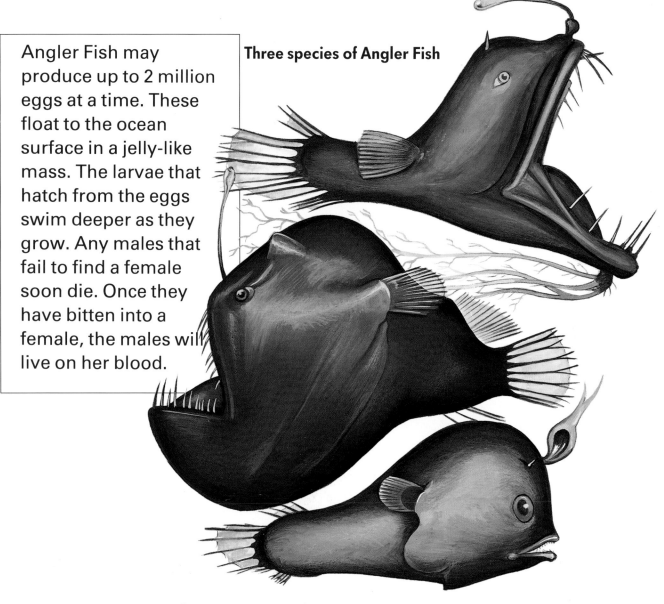

Three species of Angler Fish

Parasite and host

Some of the strangest deep-sea creatures are the Angler Fish. These tiny predators use a rod and line to catch other fish. The rod is a long and slender fin that grows out of the fish's forehead. At the end of this fin is a lure, like a fisherman's bait. This is often red and shaped like a worm. The lure tempts prey within reach of the Angler's large, teeth-filled jaws.

In some species of Angler Fish, only the females have lures. The males are much smaller than the females. Each one attaches himself to a female and lives on her as a parasite. The male feeds on material from the female's blood system. His only function is to produce sperm to fertilize her eggs.

Two males have attached themselves to this female Angler Fish ▷

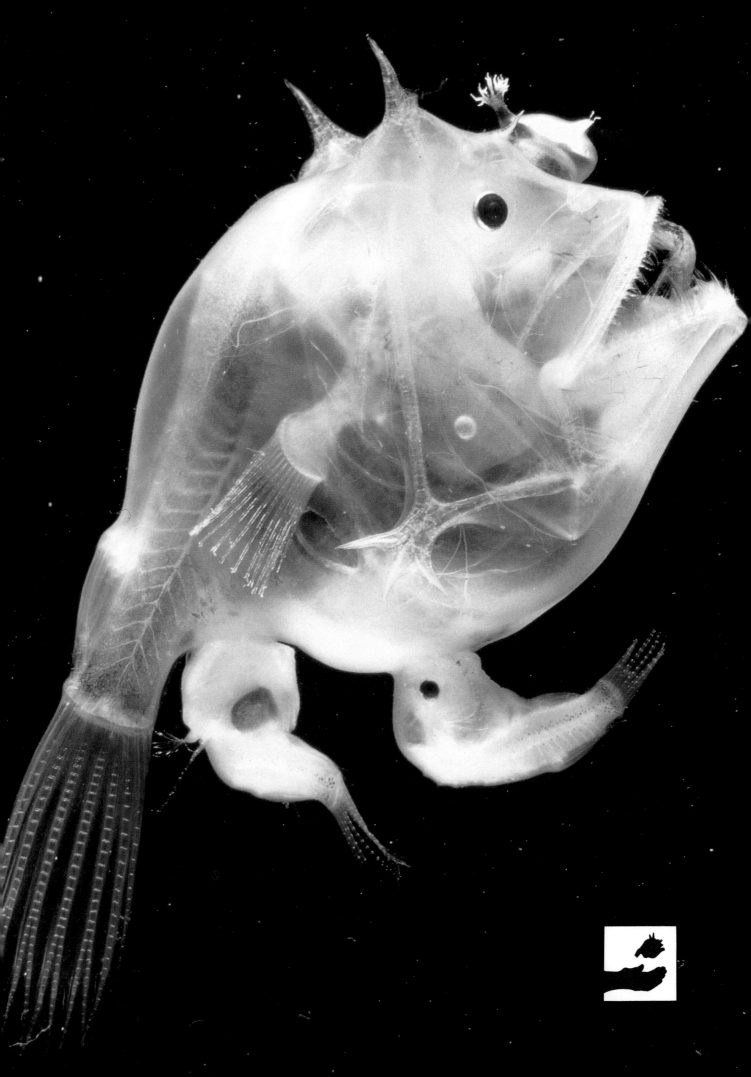

Eels

Deep-sea eels grow up to 2m (6ft) long. Like all eels they are predators, with long, thin, tapering bodies and tails. Snipe Eels have slender, flared jaws and file-like teeth. They feed on deep-sea shrimp. These Eels hang upside-down in the water and wait for their prey. When a shrimp's legs or antennae get tangled in their jaws, the eels bite their way down the prey until its whole body has been eaten.

Cut-throat Eels have huge mouths, fierce teeth and elastic stomachs. Their teeth angle inwards. This prevents any fish they catch from wriggling free. Another deep-sea eel, the Gulper Eel, has jaws that can grow to a quarter of its body length. It feeds on all kinds of small animals. The Gulper has loose sheets of skin which hang on either side of its mouth. These act like pouches, scooping food into the eel's throat when it opens its jaws.

Eel young, called larvae, look nothing like adult eels. They are transparent and shaped like a leaf or a ribbon. They can take several years to develop into adults. The larvae of most deep-sea eels live and feed close to the surface.

Gulper Eel with prey

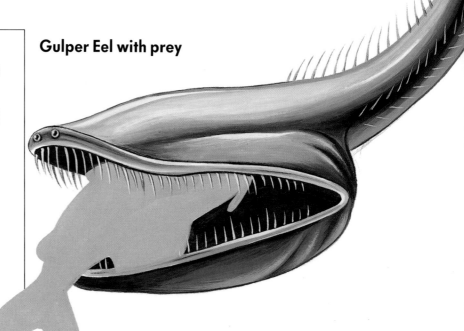

18

The Snipe Eel grows to 30cm (1ft) long ▷

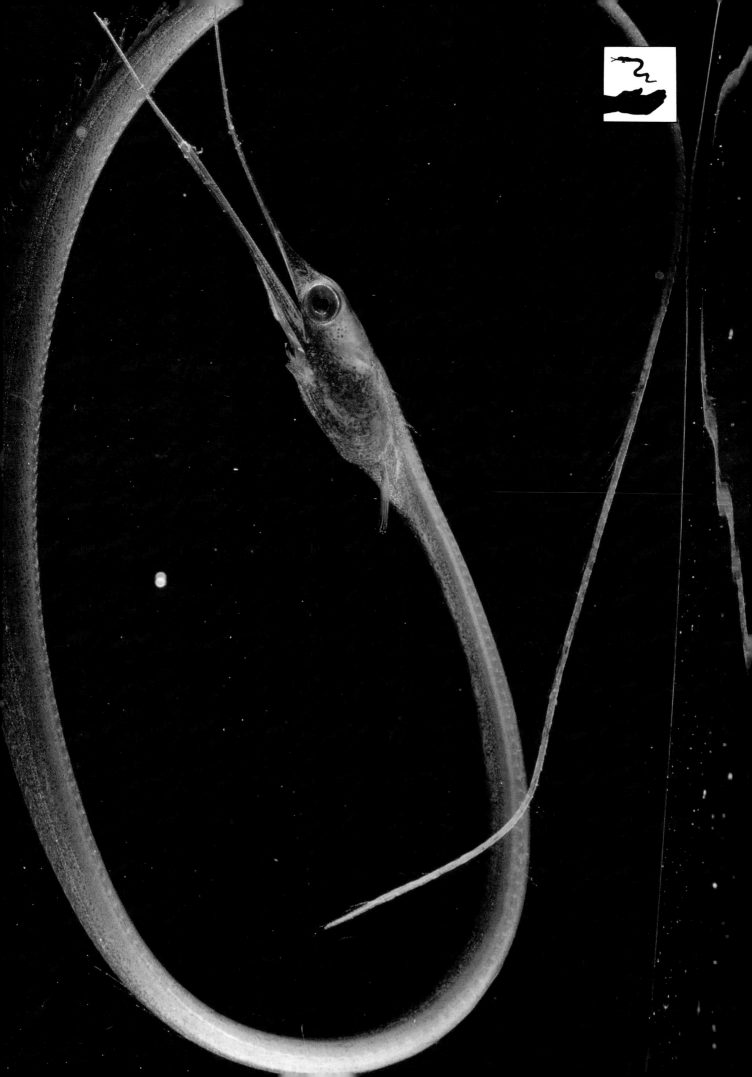

Deep divers

Male Sperm Whales are believed to dive 3 km (1.8 miles) or more under the sea. They use their strong tails to swim steadily downwards into the dark cold waters. Sometimes the whales move along the ocean floor and plough the mud for food. Usually, though, they stay still in the water and wait in ambush for squid. The Sperm Whale can stay underwater for up to 90 minutes before having to come to the surface to breathe.

The Leatherback Turtle can go for an even longer time without air – possibly up to 20 hours. But it doesn't dive so deep. This sea turtle feeds on jellyfish, snails and other soft-bodied animals. It can grow to 2.8m (9ft) long, and can swim very fast – up to 30km/h (19mph).

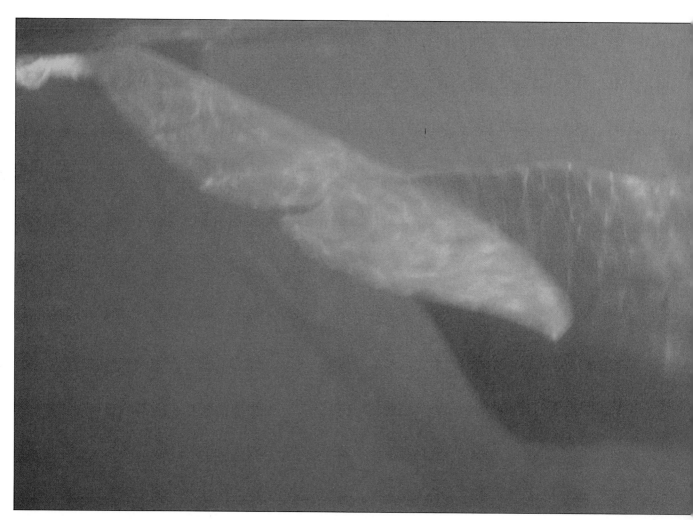

A Sperm Whale swims along near the surface △

Nautiluses are close relatives of squid and octopuses. They have a hard outer shell. They use their tentacles, which are covered in suckers, to catch fish.

Giant Squid

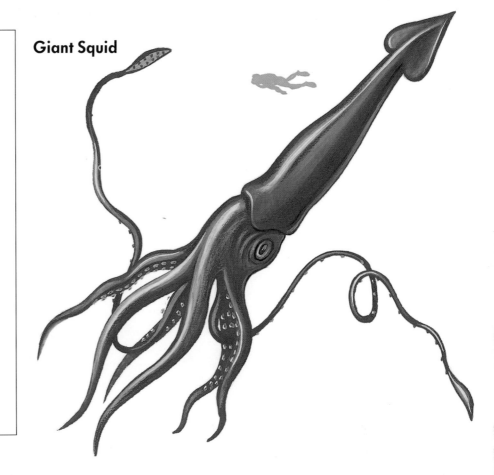

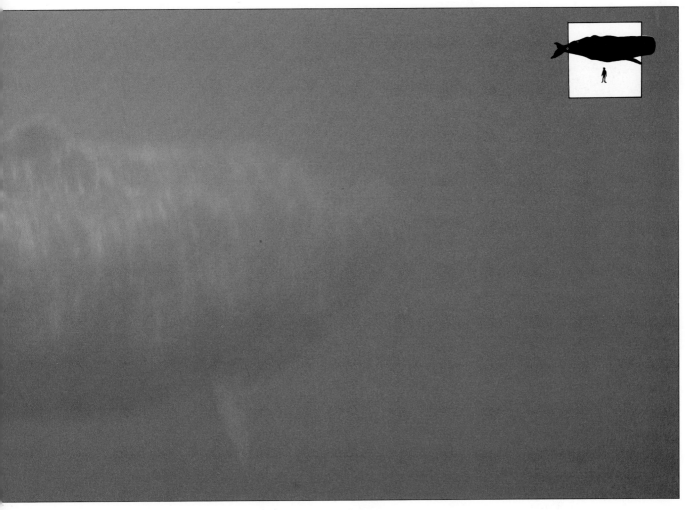

Some Rat-tail Fish squirt a jet of luminous chemicals into the water when they are threatened. The Rat-tail escapes in the cloud of light.

Three deep-sea fish that produce their own light –

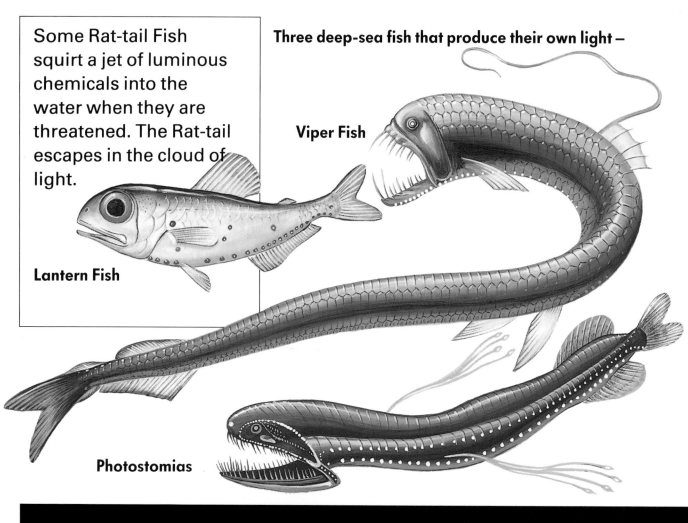

Viper Fish

Lantern Fish

Photostomias

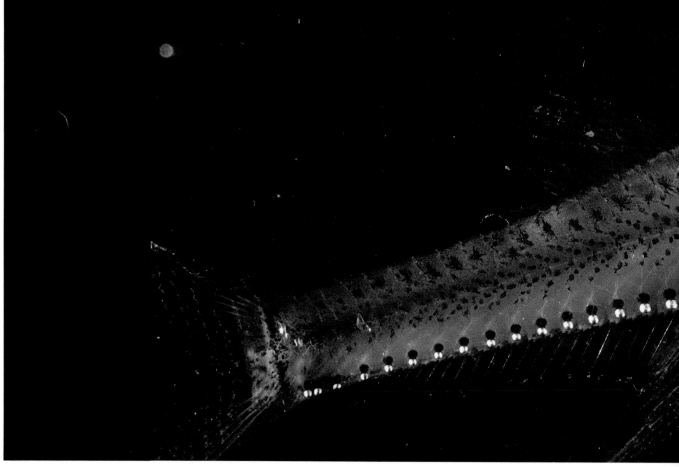

Lantern Fish have rows of lights that look like portholes on a boat △

Light-producers

Hundreds of species of deep-sea fish have their own "flashlights" – structures that glow in the dark. They use these to hunt for food or to find mates in the darkness. Lantern fish have rows of light-producing organs down the sides of their body. The glow from these organs probably disguises the fish's outline as it swims towards the surface to feed. Other lights on its body are used to attract mates.

Some species of Dragon Fish have glowing bulbs which they use as lures, in the same way that Angler Fish do. Other deep-sea fish have light organs positioned next to their eyes. These emit a red light which their eyes are highly sensitive to. They may act as searchlights to hunt for prey.

On the ocean bed

Many deep-sea creatures live buried in the mud on the ocean floor. Ragworms make burrows for protection, though they often come out to scavenge for food. Beard Worms live in long tubes that protrude from the mud. Only their head parts are exposed. The head bears up to 250 long threads, or tentacles. These are probably used both to gather food particles from the water and as gills for breathing.

Giant Tube Worms have long tentacles which they use in the same way. They live around volcanic hot water and sulphur "chimneys" which are found far below the surface. Inside the worms' bodies are bacteria that can convert sulphur substances into energy. This energy is used by both the bacteria and the worms. No other animal known to man produces energy in this way.

Beard Worm   **Worm with many tentacles**

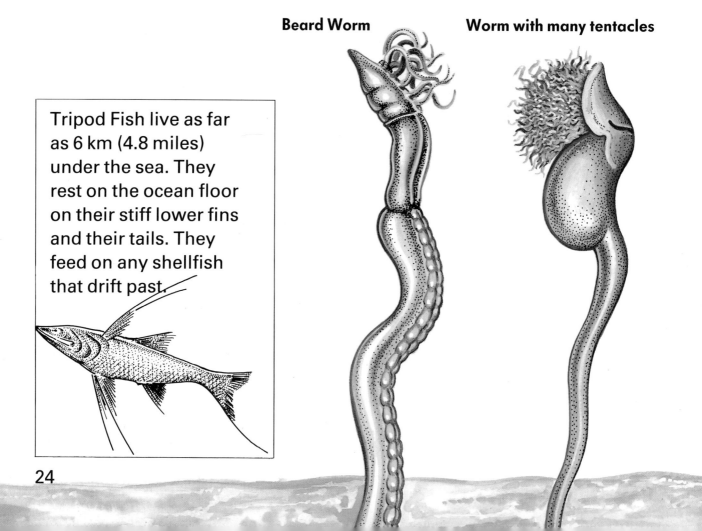

Tripod Fish live as far as 6 km (4.8 miles) under the sea. They rest on the ocean floor on their stiff lower fins and their tails. They feed on any shellfish that drift past.

Starfish and Sea Lilies

A whole family of spiny-skinned animals lives and hunts on the ocean floor. The best known members are Starfish. They have a flattened body and five or more spreading arms. On the underside of each arm are "tube-feet", like the suckers of an octopus. Starfish feed on clams, oysters and mussels. They use their tube-feet to pry open the shells of these animals and to pass the flesh towards the central mouth.

Sea Cucumbers also have tube-feet. These are arranged in a ring around the mouth, which is at one end of their sack-like body. Some species trap pieces of food with their tube-feet. Others swallow sand and mud from the ocean floor. Sea Lilies use their branching arms to strain food from the water.

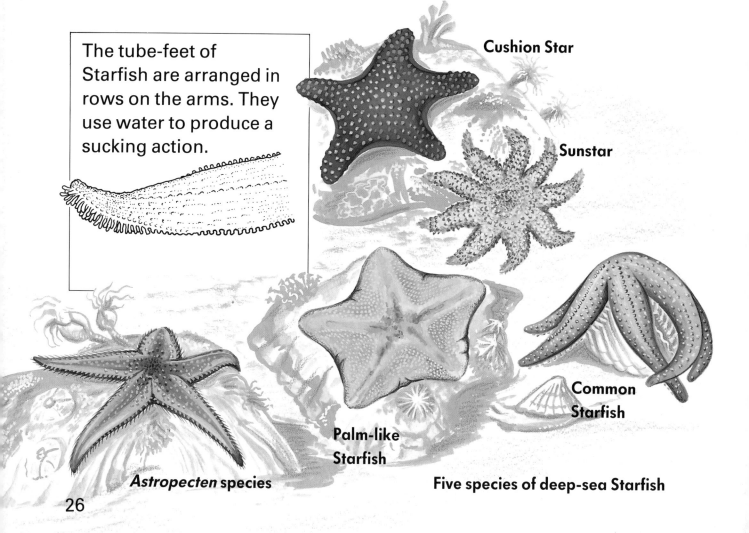

The tube-feet of Starfish are arranged in rows on the arms. They use water to produce a sucking action.

Cushion Star

Sunstar

Common Starfish

Palm-like Starfish

Astropecten species

Five species of deep-sea Starfish

Survival File

The seas and oceans of the world are enormous. Until recently people thought of them as a never-ending source of food – fish, shellfish and whales – and as a convenient dumping ground for waste. But fish populations cannot survive if too many fish are caught year after year. This overfishing also upsets the populations of plants and other animals in the oceans. The dumping of harmful chemicals and sewage into the water pollutes oceans, harming all forms of life. Even the greatest depths are now threatened.

Oil spills harm ocean life at all depths

In the last 20 years or so, special underwater craft known as submersibles and new photographic techniques have been developed. These have allowed us to explore the ocean's depths for the first time. Submersibles can go down to 5,000m (16,500ft), and recording instruments can be sent down to the ocean floor and brought back to the surface. Together, these have greatly increased our knowledge of creatures of the deep.

Many species of shark are overfished

Occasionally, fishing boats catch and haul up fish that normally live in deep waters. But many deep-sea fish have air-filled bags to help them float. When they are brought to the surface the bags expand. The fish literally explode and die the instant they are taken from the water. But even from the remains, scientists are finding that these fish may be useful sources of food and of chemicals that can combat diseases.

Nuclear debris on a Pacific island

Protecting deep-sea creatures, and indeed all ocean life, is therefore important. Nowadays, most nations of the world have agreed to restrict fishing and the dumping of hazardous materials. But oil spills and illegal dumping of waste from factories and nuclear power stations still goes on. Pesticides sprayed onto the land end up in the sea. Unless we clean up our act, many deep-sea creatures will become extinct before we can find out much about them and how they live.

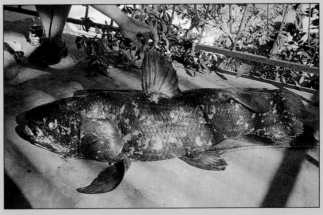

The Coelacanth, a deep-sea "living fossil"

Identification Chart

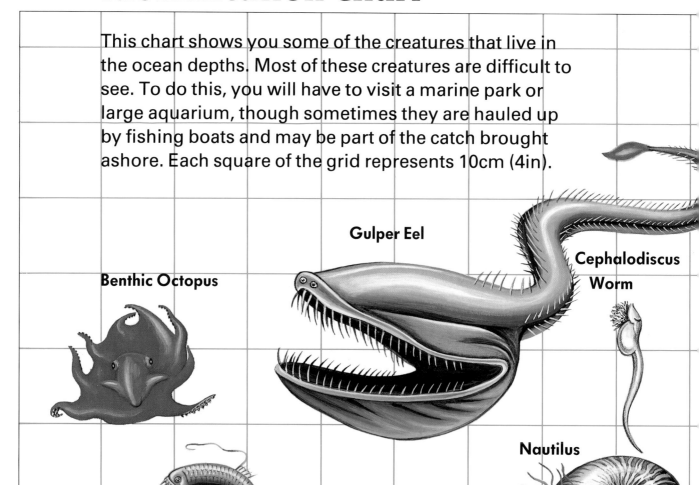

This chart shows you some of the creatures that live in the ocean depths. Most of these creatures are difficult to see. To do this, you will have to visit a marine park or large aquarium, though sometimes they are hauled up by fishing boats and may be part of the catch brought ashore. Each square of the grid represents 10cm (4in).

Gulper Eel

Cephalodiscus Worm

Benthic Octopus

Nautilus

Diretmus Fish

Viper Fish

Make your own deep-sea world

1. Using the chart above, draw the outlines of some deep-sea fish on a sheet of tracing paper.

2,3. With a black felt-tip pen and paintbrush, fill in the shapes but leave the light-producing organs white.

4. Paint around the silhouettes with a dark paint that will block the light.

5. Using cardboard supports, stand the sheet in front of a light and make the luminous organs glow.

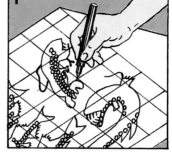

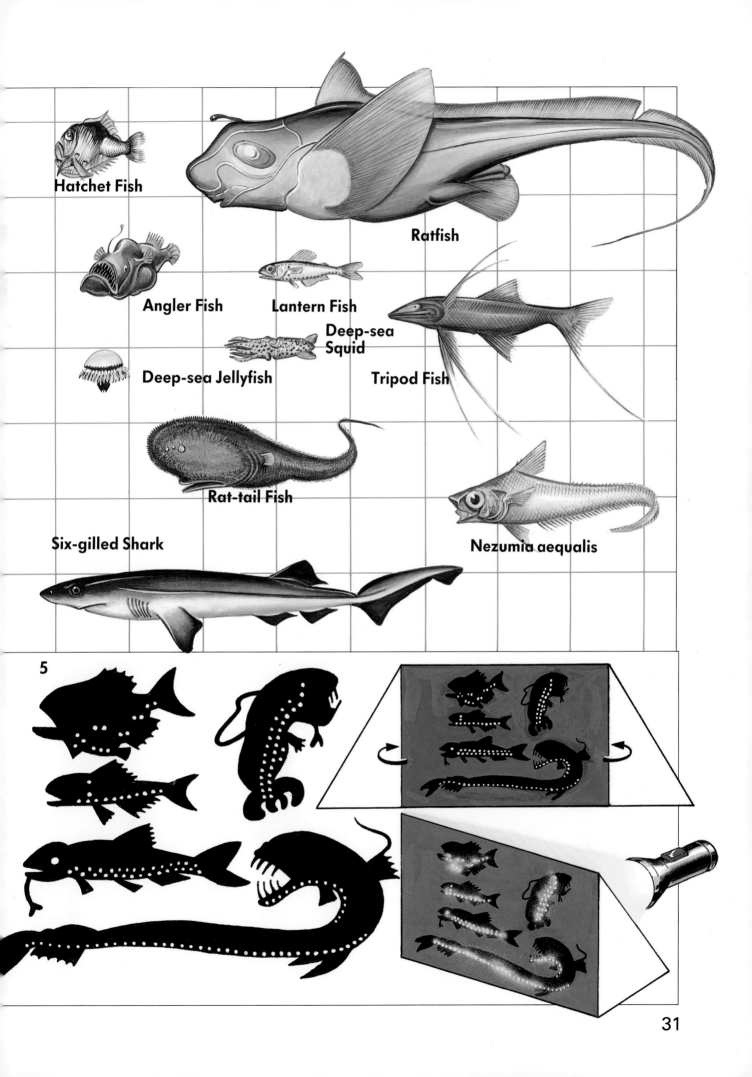

Hatchet Fish

Ratfish

Angler Fish

Lantern Fish

Deep-sea Squid

Deep-sea Jellyfish

Tripod Fish

Rat-tail Fish

Six-gilled Shark

Nezumia aequalis

5

Index